The Conference Board

Understanding
Productivity Growth

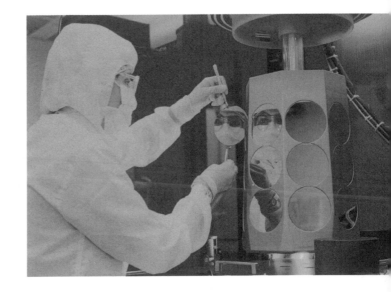

Entry, Survival, and
The Competitive Process

ing Business and Society Since 1916

The Conference Board, Inc.
845 Third Avenue
New York, NY 10022-6679
Telephone (212) 759-0900
Fax (212) 980-7014
www.conference-board.org

The Conference Board Europe
Chaussée de La Hulpe 130, bte 11
B-1000 Brussels, Belgium
Telephone (32) 2-675-5405
Fax (32) 2-675-0395
www.conference-board.org/europe.htm

The Conference Board of Canada
255 Smyth Road
Ottawa, Ontario K1H-8M7 Canada
Telephone (613) 526-3280
Fax (613) 526-4857
www.conferenceboard.ca

About The Conference Board

Founded in 1916, The Conference Board's twofold purpose is to improve the business enterprise system and to enhance the contribution of business to society.

To accomplish this, The Conference Board strives to be the leading global business membership organization that enables senior executives from all industries to explore and exchange ideas of impact on business policy and practices. To support this activity, The Conference Board provides a variety of forums and a professionally managed research program that identifies and reports objectively on key areas of changing management concern, opportunity and action.

Economic Research and Analysis

The Conference Board's economic research is highly regarded by both business and academic communities for providing a broad and interdisciplinary understanding of the forces driving the global economy and business performance. The economics program at The Conference Board provides a wide range of research and analysis on global economic issues and trends. As a result, we are an internationally recognized source of business-related research and objective indicators of economic activity. The Conference Board's economics program has been a major force in influencing business opinions and in educating the public about economic issues beginning with the production of the first continuous measure of the Cost of Living in the United States in 1919.

Today, The Conference Board publishes the widely watched indexes of Leading Economic Indicators, Consumer Confidence, Help-Wanted, Business Confidence, and Regional Performance for the major U.S. regional economies. The Economics program provides these series and thousands of other economic U.S. and international indicators in BoardView®, The Economic Information Service for Windows. The Economics Research Program also provides a wide range of analysis on subjects such as: demographics and the American consumer, the global exchange rate system, and sources of growth in productivity and living standards in industrial countries and emerging markets.

Understanding Productivity Growth
Entry, Survival, and the Competitive Process

Robert H. McGuckin, Ph.D.
Director of Economic Research
The Conference Board

Kevin J. Stiroh, Ph.D.
Economist
The Conference Board

Over the past 50 years labor productivity (output per hour) in U.S. manufacturing grew nearly 3 percent per year, easily outpacing other sectors of the U.S. economy. As many observers have pointed out, however, wide variation in performance across both time and industry lies behind this impressive record. For example, the period after 1973 was characterized by a widespread "productivity slowdown" that did not end until the 1980s, and annual manufacturing productivity growth rates across industries ranged from 1.4 to 4.4 percent between 1963 and 1992.

This study is part of a series of occasional research reports designed to analyze historical patterns of productivity and growth in order to improve our understanding of competitive process dynamics. An important aspect of this research is a focus on micro-data from the U.S. Census Bureau, rather than broader industry- or economy-wide statistics. Only by examining competition, productivity, and entry/exit patterns over extended time periods at the individual plant or firm level can one understand the sources of business success and the role of competition.

One issue of considerable interest to managers is the relative importance of new and old plants in determining productivity growth. To address this question, the present study measures the productivity performance of new entrants and long-term survivors relative to the industry average from 1963 to 1992.[1] Since new entrants compete with existing plants to advance the productivity frontier, managers must understand the fundamentals of successful competition to gauge their own relative performance and evaluate future prospects.

A "vintage effect" measures the productivity advantage of new plants with access to the latest capital, organization structure, and expertise. Average vintage gains were substantial—more recent entrants show 2.0 percent higher productivity each year relative to earlier entrants. A "survival effect" measures the increase in productivity of surviving plants due to such factors as learning-by-doing and economies of scale. Productivity grew 2.3 percent per year for manufacturing plants that began production between 1963 and 1967, and survived until 1992.

Primary Conclusions

- Expansion of the productivity frontier is driven by the competitive interaction between successful incumbents and new entrants.

- New plants have 2.0 percent annual productivity gains relative to earlier entrants.

- Successful plants at birth tend to remain successful and survive.

- Plants born in the mid-1960s and surviving until the early 1990s averaged productivity growth of 2.3 percent per year.

- The "productivity slowdown" affected both incumbent and new plants.

- The competitive process is pervasive, but varies greatly across industries.

- High-tech industries experience faster productivity growth and new entrants are immediately competitive.

---

[1] This work will also form the basis for examining the 1990s when the data become available.

These forces are clearly important sources of productivity growth, as new plants continuously enter with better equipment and technology, while incumbents gain experience and knowledge. Both factors, however, show considerable variation over time. For example, there is a clear slowdown in survival gains during the 1972 to 1982 period, followed by a return to rapid growth after 1982. This flattening of the survival curve coincides with the much-discussed productivity slowdown in the U.S. economy. Perhaps more surprising, vintage improvements were also relatively small over this period. That is, new plants experienced the same slowdown, indicating that both old and new plants were affected by the productivity slowdown.

At each point in time, however, these two factors roughly offset each other and the data show a "convergence" in productivity levels of plants that began producing in different years. In 1992, for example, there was little difference in the productivity levels of plants established at different times between 1967 and 1987. This convergence strongly suggests that the competitive process drives productivity growth as successful plants—both incumbents and new entrants—jointly expand the frontier to increase industry productivity.[2] To understand how this interaction shapes their industry, managers must be aware of the importance of these factors in their particular industry.

Evidence shows that the competitive process is pervasive across manufacturing, but that the magnitude and relative importance of vintage and survival gains vary substantially across industries, particularly with respect to technology levels. From 1963 to 1992, for example, Scientific Instrument plants, a high-tech industry,

Table 1

Structure of the Cohort Data

Cohort	Entry Years
1963	Before 1963
1967	1963–67
1972	1968–72
1977	1973–77
1982	1978–82
1987	1983–87
1992	1988–92

Source: The Conference Board.

---

[2] These results are based on the working paper, "The Impact of Vintage and Survival on Productivity: Evidence from Cohorts of U.S. Manufacturing Plants," by J. Bradford Jensen, Robert H. McGuckin, and Kevin J. Stiroh.

Data and Methodology

The Longitudinal Research Database (LRD), maintained by the U.S. Census Bureau, is a comprehensive database that includes all manufacturing plants operating in any of the following years: 1963, 1967, 1972, 1977, 1982, 1987, and 1992. It contains fundamental production variables such as the value of output and capital, employment, and descriptive statistics identifying a plant's detailed industry, location, owners, etc. As summarized in Table 1, seven cohorts were created based on entry year for each of the 19 two-digit SIC industries that cover the entire manufacturing sector.

Table 2 on page 5 details the structure of the data and presents summary statistics. Each column represents a point in time from 1963 to 1992, and each row represents a different set of plants. The "Industry" row includes all plants operating in the LRD in a particular period; the "New Plants" row includes all plants that entered in that period; and the "Cohort" rows include all plants that entered in a particular period and survived through 1992. The upper panel reports the number of plants and the lower panel reports average (hour-weighted) labor productivity, defined as value-added per hour worked, for each group.

In 1967, for example, there were 184,300 plants in the LRD and 50,000 of them entered between 1963 and 1967. Of these 50,000 new entrants, approximately 7,600 survived through 1992 and they comprise the 1967 cohort. These surviving plants increased productivity from $29.8 per hour worked in 1967 to $53.3 in 1992. Over the same period, average productivity for all plants increased from $28.3 per hour worked in 1967 to $54.0 in 1992. In 1992, 82,500 new plants entered and show the lowest 1992 productivity—a mere $45.0 per hour. This because they only entered recently and low productivity plants have yet to be weeded out.

showed productivity growth of 4.4 percent per year, while those in Primary Metal Products, a medium-tech industry, managed annual gains of only 1.4 percent. More broadly, high-tech industries as a group experienced faster productivity growth, larger vintage gains, and a stronger tendency toward convergence across cohorts of different ages. In medium- and low-tech industries, on the other hand, older plants dominate and there is less evidence of rapid convergence across cohorts.

These findings reflect fundamental differences in production processes across the industrial spectrum: New firms can immediately be competitive in high-tech industries, while older, larger firms tend to dominate in others. As powerful vintage and survival factors interact to raise the competitive threshold, they provide a useful benchmark of success that varies across industries. Managers must be able to match the productivity gains in their particular industry to be successful and survive.

> Examining competition, productivity, and entry/exit patterns over extended time periods can help explain the sources of business success.

Table 2
Descriptive Statistics for Cohorts of U.S. Manufacturing Plants, 1963–92

	1963	1967	1972	1977	1982	1987	1992
Number of Plants (000s)							
Industry	301.1	184.3	186.1	196.6	213.8	197.9	221.5
New Plants	301.1	50.0	67.1	71.9	77.2	63.5	82.5
Cohorts of Plants That Survived to 1992							
	31.3	7.6	12.1	16.7	23.2	34.3	82.5
		31.3	7.6	12.1	16.7	23.2	34.3
			31.3	7.6	12.1	16.7	23.2
				31.3	7.6	12.1	16.7
					31.3	7.6	12.1
						31.3	7.6
							31.3
Average Labor Productivity							
Industry	25.2	28.3	33.1	35.2	38.3	48.3	54.0
New Plants	25.2	23.7	28.3	28.3	30.5	41.4	45.0
Cohorts of Plants That Survived to 1992							
	30.4	29.8	34.0	32.1	33.3	44.6	45.0
		33.7	34.4	34.6	36.7	44.6	51.4
			38.9	36.6	38.4	45.5	53.6
				41.0	39.4	48.4	49.3
					44.3	50.2	52.7
						55.6	53.3
							60.8

Note: Average Labor Productivity is defined as value-added per hour worked.
All productivity estimates are employment-weighted averages across all manufacturing industries.

Source: The Conference Board; Longitudinal Research Database, U.S. Census Bureau.

Recent Vintages Are More Productive

At least since Robert Solow's work in 1960, economists have observed fundamental differences in the production techniques and capital equipment of plants from different eras, and have recognized they have a large impact on productivity.[3] Moreover, these differences have been used as the basis for sophisticated models that study business cycles and other economic issues.[4] Thus, a plant's entry period or "vintage" should be a good predictor of its relative productivity.

To weigh the evidence for a vintage effect—higher productivity in more recent entrants—productivity levels of successive generations (cohorts) of new plants were compared. By focusing on new plants, age-related gains (e.g., plants may grow and achieve economies of scale after entry) that might obscure fundamental differences in initial productivity across vintages are eliminated. In practice, this means that only plants less than five years old were included in a cohort.

For manufacturing as a whole, a strong vintage effect exists since each cohort of new plants is more productive than earlier ones. For each year from 1963 to 1992, Chart 1 shows the log of productivity of new entrants and the contemporaneous industry average. Between 1963 and 1992, the mean vintage gain was 57.1 percent, or nearly 2.0 percent per year. Even when more sophisticated econometrics were introduced to control for other factors, there were strong and significant vintage gains. For instance, the 1992 vintage was 46.8 percent more productive on average than the 1963 vintage, after controlling for differences in labor quality, capital intensity, and general time-related factors affecting the productivity of all plants. The average vintage effect from 1963 to 1992 for each industry is reported in Table 3.

These results provide several interesting insights. First, initial productivity is a crucial determinant of success and survival. Although new cohorts entered with productivity above earlier cohorts (the vintage effect), their productivity was still below the contemporaneous industry average. Plants that

Chart 1
The Vintage Effect
Productivity of Industry and New Vintages in Entry Years

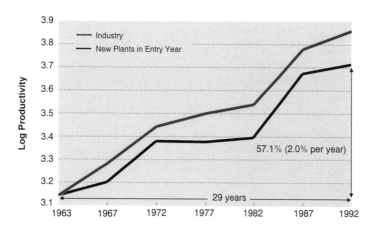

Note: All estimates are the average of log of labor productivity (value-added per hour worked) for 19 manufacturing industries.

3   Robert M. Solow, "Investment and Technical Progress," in Kenneth Arrow, Samuel Karlin, and Paul Suppres, eds., *Mathematical Methods in the Social Sciences* (Stanford, CA: Stanford University Press, 1960).

4   Ricardo Caballero and Mohammed Hammour, "The Cleansing Effects of Recessions," *American Economic Review* 84, (1994), pp. 1356–68; Russell Cooper, John Haltiwanger, and Laura Power, "Machine Replacement and the Business Cycle: Lumps and Bumps," NBER Working Paper #5260 (1995).

survived through 1992, however, entered with high productivity relative to plants that failed, enabling them to withstand the competitive process and survive for a long period. Second, even new entrants were not immune to the well-documented productivity slowdown of the 1970s and early 1980s. The relatively small vintage gains in this period suggest that the slowdown was pervasive and not limited to older plants that may have been hardest hit by the energy shocks of the 1970s.

Table 3
Productivity Growth Rates for U.S. Manufacturing Industries

SIC Code	Industry	Technology Class	Industry	New Vintages	1967 Cohort
20, 21	Food and Tobacco	3	2.57	1.96	2.19
22	Textiles	3	3.62	3.66	3.30
23	Apparel	3	2.73	2.06	3.88
24	Lumber and Wood	3	1.80	1.43	1.70
25	Furniture	3	2.05	1.71	1.52
26	Paper	3	2.55	1.93	2.73
27	Printing and Publishing	3	1.64	1.04	2.14
28	Chemical	1	3.16	2.59	1.91
29	Petroleum	2	1.75	0.06*	2.12
30	Rubber	2	2.27	1.90	2.18
31	Leather	3	2.25	1.73	1.70
32	Stone, Clay, and Glass	2	1.76	1.39	1.83
33	Primary Metal Products	2	1.36*	0.99	1.43
34	Fabricated Metal Products	2	1.51	1.33	1.35*
35	Industrial Machinery	1	2.71	2.47	2.16
36	Electric Machinery	1	4.28	3.93**	4.28**
37	Transportation	1	2.08	1.77	1.47
38	Scientific Instruments	1	4.36**	3.46	3.72
39	Miscellaneous Manufacturing	2	2.60	2.02	1.59
	Simple Mean		2.47	1.97	2.27
	Weighted Mean		2.63	2.00	2.33
	Simple Mean for 5 High-tech Industries		3.32	2.85	2.71
	Simple Mean for 6 Medium-tech Industries		1.88	1.28	1.75
	Simple Mean for 8 Low-tech Industries		2.39	1.94	2.39

Note: Technology is classified as: 1 (high-tech), 2 (medium-tech), and 3 (low-tech), as defined by the OECD. All growth rates are annual averages.

* signifies the minimum and ** signifies the maximum.

Industry is the growth in productivity for all plants in industry from 1963 to 1992.
New Vintages is the Vintage Effect: growth in productivity of new entrants from 1963 to 1992.
1967 Cohort is the Survival Effect: growth in productivity of the 1967 cohort from 1967 to 1992.

Source: The Conference Board; Longitudinal Research Database, U.S. Census Bureau.

Increasing Productivity With Age

There are many possible explanations why surviving manufacturing plants become more productive with age. Some argue that managers and workers improve their skills with experience and become more efficient as they produce more (learning-by-doing).[5] A related view holds that, because plants tend to grow larger with age, economies of scale may allow them to become more productive.

Productivity growth may also contain a random component (such as unforeseen events, management error, or luck) that causes some plants to improve and others to decline.[6] Lucky plants may have temporarily high productivity and survive, while unlucky plants experience low productivity, exit the industry, and drop from the sample. Age and productivity, therefore, may be empirically related without the type of causal relationship implied in learning-by-doing models. Since the available data do not enable us to separately identify these factors, we combine the impact into a single "survival effect" that measures the change in productivity as a cohort ages.

The survival effect is quite large as manufacturing plants in the 1967 cohort became 56.9 percent more productive from their time of entry to 1992. Chart 2 plots the log of productivity for these plants from 1967 to 1992 and the contemporaneous industry average. Since the 1967 cohort is a balanced sample that traces the interaction between age, selection, and productivity over a relatively long period, it is the primary focus in this report. The results for other cohorts are consistent with those reported for 1967, and Table 3 on page 7 shows the survival effect from 1967 to 1992 for the 1967 cohort from each manufacturing industry.

While survival gains generally occur contemporaneously with industry-wide gains, plants also raised productivity relative to the industry in the 5 to 10 years immediately following entry. This suggests that a random process is not the sole cause of the survival effect, since a truly random process would not lead to differential growth rates in the first 10 years. A strong survival effect was also

Chart 2
The Survival Effect
Productivity of Industry and 1967 Surviving Cohort

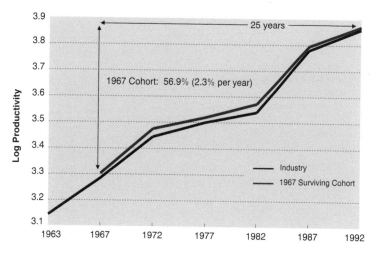

Note: All estimates are the average of log of labor productivity (value-added per hour worked) for 19 manufacturing industries.

5 Byong-Hyong Bahk and Michael Gort, "Decomposing Learning by Doing in New Plants," *Journal of Political Economy*, Vol. 101, No. 4. (1993), pp. 561-83; Eric J. Bartlesman and Mark Doms, "Understanding Productivity: Lessons from Longitudinal Micro Data sets," manuscript (1997).

6 Martin N. Baily, Charles Hulten, and David Campbell, "The Distribution of Productivity in Manufacturing Plants, *Brookings Papers: Microeconomics* (1992), pp. 187-249; Boyan Jovanovic, "Selection and the Evolution of Industry," *Econometrica*, Vol. 50, No. 3 (1982), pp. 649-70; G. Steven Olley and Ariel Pakes, "The Dynamics of Productivity in the Telecommunications Equipment Industry," *Econometrica*, Vol. 64, No. 6 (1996), pp. 1263-97.

confirmed by more sophisticated econometrics that control for the impact of labor quality, capital intensity, and industry-wide factors. This means managers cannot entirely avoid the learning process simply by hiring skilled workers or heavily investing in new capital. Rather, hands-on-learning and accumulated expertise are important contributors to success that must be experienced through the production process.

Vintage and Survival Trade-Off

Plant vintage and survival are both good predictors of relative productivity. At each point in time, however, they work in opposite directions, leading to a "net effect." It is an empirical matter whether older or younger plants are more productive—i.e., new cohorts gain from a more modern technology and capital, while older cohorts enjoy the benefits of experience, age, and scale. Since competition makes it hard for low productivity plants of any age to survive, there is no fundamental reason to expect the net effect of vintage and survival to be either positive or negative.

Chart 3 plots the productivity of each cohort in 1992 relative to the 1992 industry average. The data show that these two forces roughly offset each other, since there is little difference in productivity across cohorts in 1992, except for the 1992 cohort itself. This implies that the competitive forces driving entry and exit also control the trade-off and lead the two effects to roughly balance each other. The six cohorts that entered prior to 1987 are typically within 5 percent of the average productivity of the industry, and statistical tests show that observed differences are insignificant. Moreover, after controlling for differences in labor quality and capital intensity, no significant relationship between a plant's cohort and its relative productivity emerges. Similar results were also found for 1987.

The obvious outlier in Chart 3, the 1992 cohort, is significantly below the industry average. As noted above, this reflects the exit process—many low productivity plants in the 1992 cohort have not been in the industry long enough to have been forced out by the competitive process. Additional analysis suggests that much of this shortfall can be attributed to lower labor quality and less capital-intensive operations for the youngest plants, which prevent them from achieving industry-wide productivity levels. To succeed, management must be aware of the strong relationship between labor quality, capital intensity, productivity, and survival.

Chart 3
The Net Effect
Productivity of Surviving Cohorts Relative to Industry in 1992

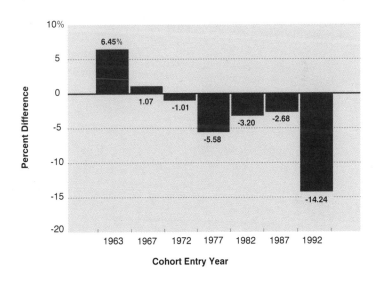

Note: All estimates are the average difference between the log of labor productivity (value-added per hour worked) of each cohort and the industry.

These findings broadly describe the underlying competitive process in which vintage gains, survival patterns, and age-related gains interact to determine the productivity frontier. Although new and incumbent plants influence each other in their struggle to survive, we cannot identify the exact causal mechanism behind the productivity gains with the data currently available. Are new plants and their advanced technologies forcing older plants to evolve and catch-up? Or, are existing plants becoming more productive and allowing only the best new plants to enter?[7] Because the data only reveal the outcome of this interaction we cannot be sure, but the implications are clear. The competitive process extends the productivity frontier and all plants, incumbents and entrants alike, must match these productivity gains to survive.

High-Tech Industries and More Rapid Change

The final portion of this report examines the vintage and survival effects for different manufacturing industries. The 19 industries examined were classified as either high-, medium-, or low-tech, according to definitions created by the Organization for Economic Cooperation and Development (OECD). These classifications are based on the amount of research and development expenditure embodied in the output of each industry, yielding five high-, six medium-, and eight low-tech industries. Table 3 on page 7 lists the technology classification for each industry and the simple means of productivity growth rates for each grouping.

The vintage effect, while positive for all technology groups, is much larger in the high-tech industries. In 1992, new high-tech plants were 82.7 percent more productive on average than new plants in 1963.[8] Electric Machinery, a high-tech industry that produces semi-conductors and other electronic goods, showed the largest vintage gains—a 114.0 percent advantage for the 1992 cohort relative to the 1963 cohort in their respective entry years—while Petroleum, a medium-tech industry, showed a cumulative vintage effect of only 1.7 percent. Moreover, high-tech industries showed more rapid productivity growth in general, due in part to a stronger vintage effect.

Although positive in all sectors, survival gains were also largest in high-tech industries. The average 1967 high-tech cohort experienced a 67.8 percent productivity gain between 1967 and 1992, while medium- and low-tech cohorts averaged 43.8 and 59.8 percent gains, respectively. Industries with the largest survival gains, however, were not all high-tech—the 1967 cohort in Apparel (low-tech) posted a 97.0 percent productivity gain through 1992.

Managers cannot entirely avoid the learning process simply by hiring skilled workers or heavily investing in new capital.

---

[7] In addition, the data cannot identify whether the new plants were true start-ups or were developed by firms already in existence.

[8] Corresponding differences in medium- and low-tech industries were 37.1 and 56.3 percent, respectively.

In contrast to the similarities in the vintage and survival profiles, net effects varied greatly across technology groups. Chart 4 is similar to Chart 3 on page 9, but breaks out the net effect for the three technology classes. High-tech industries, for example, tend toward convergence with no obvious productivity pattern across cohorts, while medium- and low-tech industries systematically show older cohorts to be more productive than more recent ones. Thus, there is a general tendency for the survival effect to dominate the vintage effect in low- and medium-tech industries, but not in high-tech.

These results shed light on the fundamental differences in production modes across manufacturing industries. Petroleum, for example, is very scale-oriented and shows small vintage gains, but strong survival gains for older cohorts. This suggests that it takes time for newer Petroleum plants to reach a competitive scale. In Electric Machinery, on the other hand, vintage gains are relatively large and recent entrants are not at a productivity disadvantage. Again, this reflects the nature of production in the electronics industry, where rapid technological change allows new plants to immediately become competitive and places increasing pressure on older plants to improve productivity in order to survive.

Concluding Observations

Productivity growth, a fundamental part of successful business operations, has obvious implications for competitiveness and profitability. The process, however, is not well understood and a great deal of variation exists across industries and over time. These results describe the experience of U.S. manufacturing plants from 1963 to 1992 and offer insight into the processes that determine business success.

Successful plants enter with relatively high productivity, but must also constantly improve to survive and remain competitive. As new plants enter with better capital or state-of-the-art technology and incumbent plants learn, evolve, and adapt, the productivity frontier is steadily pushed outward. Although the pace and timing vary across industries, the fundamental process has the same implications for all businesses—only plants that consistently evolve and match these productivity gains will be successful and survive.

Chart 4

High-, Medium-, and Low-Tech Net Effect

High-Tech Industries
Cohort Relative to Industry Average in 1992

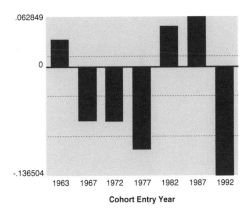

Medium-Tech Industries
Cohort Relative to Industry Average in 1992

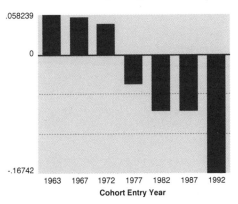

Low-Tech Industries
Cohort Relative to Industry Average in 1992

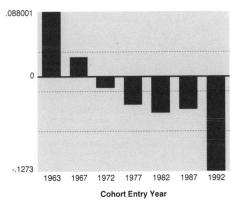